Bottle Cutting

Bottle Cutting

by Michael De Forrest

GALAHAD BOOKS · NEW YORK

The author wishes to thank Louis A. Schreiber of Stylecraft *Division of L. Gordon & Son, Inc., distributors of "Ephrem's Olde Time Bottle Cutter," for assistance and advice in the preparation of this book. Also Carol Plaine and Marilyn Houston of Pyramid Publications, who thought it might be a good idea and helped significantly to make it a better one.*

Bottle Cutting

CONTENTS

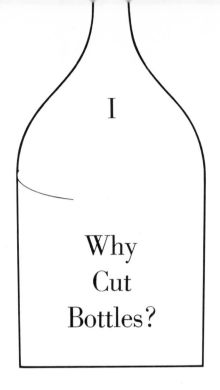

I

Why Cut Bottles?

"You can't make a silk purse out of a sow's ear," my great aunt used to observe from time to time, and right enough she was. Her version of the adage, however, ended with a spirited qualification, "but it sure ought to be good for something." It had a blunt, homespun quality that today makes me think of warm, sleepy afternoons and lumpy cinnamon-dusted applesauce spooned up in a flood of cold milk, and of the roomy, busy kitchen that was part laboratory, part literary salon, and always the scene of everyday miracles in which scraps of fabric got stitched into quilts or braided into rugs, where flowers were dried for winter bouquets and a week's harvest of fat scarlet tomatoes became a year's supply of the world's best ketchup.

Wise enough not to court disappointment by trying to fashion a silk purse from anything but a bit of silk, my aunt was an arch

foe of waste. She would have loved cutting bottles. Not only because she actively disapproved of waste but also because she enjoyed finding attractive use for what otherwise might have been meaningless clutter, worthless junk, or troublesome garbage. If anyone could have told her how five minutes' work would transform an empty wine bottle into a hanging planter, she would have given him a medal of honor—or a brown-edge cookie, which would have been an even better reward. But no matter how enthusiastic she might have been, she never would have lost sight of the realities of the situation. The satisfaction of converting empty bottles into tumblers, funnels, lampshades and the like never would have made her deceive herself into thinking that from "No Deposit/No Return" soda bottles she was creating glass objects that would rival the fine fire of Waterford crystal, the perfection of costly Steuben glass, or the artistic triumphs of Tiffany's masterworks. So although she never would have invited her cut-bottle tumblers to serve at a company dinner when the dining table would be leafed out to its maximum dimensions and snowed in under heirloom damask, she would have been the first to press them into service for a five o'clock lemonade amid the cool, plant-packed shadows of the side porch. She would have offered them proudly there, and enthusiastically related how her new hobby had resulted in that set of generously proportioned emerald-green glasses that hadn't cost a penny. And if by chance a glass was broken, she would have smiled and said, "Now be careful how you pick up the pieces and don't cut yourself, and we'll go and find ourselves another bottle and cut us a free replacement."

Cut bottles can be made into practical, attractive, tasteful articles that substantially enhance one's pleasure in many situations. It is, for example, infinitely nicer to keep your pencils in a pretty jar of cobalt-blue glass than in an old cardboard box. For one thing, it makes for a neater, more attractive desk. Plus which, there's a lot to be said for the fringe benefits derived from having pleasant, even beautiful accessories to see us through what we too often tend to dismiss as "everyday life." It is, after all, everyday life that most of us live every day, and unless you happen to subscribe to some ultra-Spartan code, there's no prohibition against making every day as agreeable and attractive as possible. Most of us couldn't afford to press a Baccarat tumbler, or an old mold-patterned jelly dish into service as a pencil jar. But anyone with five minutes to spare, a bottle-cutting kit, a whisper of patience and an empty Bromo bottle can have a neat one practically free of charge. And the ecologists' beaming approval into the bargain. Perhaps even more satisfying would be the joy of having created something, however simple or utilitarian, at a time when prepared, prefabricated, prepunched, predrawn projects have all but eliminated that pleasure. Not everyone can paint a picture, or restore an antique grandfather's clock. But with the new bottle-cutting kits, absolutely anyone can transform almost any old bottle into an astonishing choice of beautiful, useful and inexpensive objects that can be duplicated *ad infinitum* and replaced at no, or extremely modest, cost.

Economy

Want a whole new set of cocktail glasses for your next big party? At a cost of absolutely nothing you could collect old beer or soda bottles and cut them into enough glasses to see you through the largest bash. You even could have enough glasses in reserve to forget all about washing up during the party, or marking each glass, as one hostess annoyingly used to do. (No matter how many little stickers and tags she used, someone always got mixed up and conversation pretty much boiled down to "Is this your glass or mine?") And after the party if you didn't feel up to washing all those glasses, you could trundle them off to the glass-recycling center and dispose of them with a clear conscience. Comes your next big *soirée*, you simply create a fresh stock of free glasses. And you will have a very delightful time doing it, too.

Same goes for serving dishes for a cookout, or for the kids ice-cream party, for instance. The bottom of a 38-ounce size salad-oil bottle yields a just-right glass saucer that won't get all guggy like a cardboard plate and won't split or fly away at a breath like a plastic one.

You can use them everyday, too. For a temporary residence—a student apartment, for example—cut-bottle tableware provides an excellent no-cost solution. When it's time to vacate for vacation, or to move on to the next post, there's no bother of packing and expense of storing or shipping glasses and glassware. Chuck them at the nearest glass-collection point and start from scratch with a fresh batch of bottles and your trusty cutting device.

The "No Deposit/No Return" legend that marks many commercial bottles today can be a convenience as well as a nuisance, for while the nonrefillable bottle has become a source of concern

to the environmentalists, the dedicated bottle-cutter can transform it into a nonreturnable container for candies, cookies, flower arrangements, homemade jams and jellies, preserved fruits, pickles, spreads, dips, whatever seems in order when gift time rolls around.

And what gift could be more cheerful and less expensive than a living garden under glass, with dwarf plants thriving in a bottle-cut terrarium? For the home gardener—indoor or outdoor variety—the voice of experience vows there's no better or more convenient way to see seedlings off to a flourishing start than to set them in one of these cost-free miniature greenhouses. Now that hanging planters again are all the rage, how about cutting some bottles into single or multiple containers to be given with a rooted start of your favorite ivy, philodendron, or begonia?

Or some handsome new hanging lamps—single drops or multiples limited only by your space and imagination—for the cost of a few feet of electric wire, a socket, a plug, and occasionally, a bottle cork and a bit of threaded pipe? At perhaps two dollars a unit, your cut-bottle fixtures will rival store-bought imports going for ten times as much. And if one day you decide that it would please you to turn in your green shades for a set in amber or aqua or royal blue or smoky yellow or peach or . . . you can have a brand-new color scheme in just about as much time as it takes to say "custom made."

Ecology

Communities throughout the country have established recycling centers with bins for glass reclamation. Ecologically concerned and civic-minded organizations are waging collection drives to properly dispose of surplus glass even as they once did to compensate for wartime shortages of tin cans and scrap metals. Beverage companies are impressing their containers with legends urging the customer to dispose of the bottle properly. Several have even incorporated an ecological message into their advertising campaigns and have pegged television commercials to correct disposal of their disposable bottles. Concern over the monumental litter of empty and broken bottles seems to be mounting in all quarters and is in no way mollified by a switch to plastic containers, which are an even greater environmental problem, since they do not lend themselves to recycling. And the more the authorities cite the magnitude of the situation, the more many individuals feel frustrated that whatever their efforts, they cannot possibly contribute anything significant toward the improvement of the situation.

Untrue!

By reclaiming and recycling waste—and that's what all those empty bottles would be if the bottle cutter weren't converting them into useful and attractive objects—you can score a bold stroke in favor of environmental improvement. Moreover, by introducing others to this fascinating and fulfilling hobby, you encourage them to do the same. And you can set a super example by regularly gathering broken pieces and unused elements and trundling them off to the recycling center. You also help to discourage the use of those troublesome plastic containers, since any passionate bottle cutter automatically will reach for the product available in beautiful recyclable glass.

Enjoyment

Probably the best reason for doing anything is that you really find pleasure in it. The bottles and the precision-instrument look of the cutting tools has lifted bottle cutting out of the routine hobby-craft category to emerge as something of a new national pastime to be enjoyed by one and all.

There's no reason why a youngster able to handle other household tools responsibly couldn't enjoy cutting bottles. And he's no more likely to have an accident than he would wielding a hammer. In fact, less likely. Broken glass is a nuisance to clean up, but most of the breakage in bottle cutting occurs in transportation, cleaning, or disposal. I have cracked bottles while attempting to cut them, but I have never had one shatter at any point in the cutting process. And no one, of any age, has to get involved with sharp edges, glass dust and the like. No one, that is, with a bottle cutter, some glasses or goggles, and even a shred of common sense.

Happily, bottle cutting is a unisex hobby. More and more hobbies are getting there, but bottle cutting has appealed to male and female alike since the first kits came on the market.

So praise be the bottle-cutting kits! When they claim to be easy to assemble and easier to use, believe it or not, they're telling the truth! Of several available kits one even is sold in preassembled, ready-to-use form. If you have found through bitter experience that all things are not what copywriters would have them seem, try bottle cutting and have your faith at least partially restored. It actually is just as simple, as safe, and as much fun as they say it is. If possible, it's more.

Try your wings — and your new skills — on some simple projects, just for openers. None of the useful objects on the following pages requires more than one easily completed cut. All were made from commercial bottles.

Quart soda bottle cut
below the shoulder yields
Swedish-modern vase.

Wine-jug Bowl

The puffy border of grapes impressed around the base of a domestic wine bottle adds decorative interest to a bowl cut just where the plain glass of the funnel-shaped top merges with the patterned area. Be sure to score such a bottle where it is smooth.

Bubble-glass Planter

*Hobnail pattern
of gin bottle called
for very careful
scoring (above, as a
planter; at right,
as a chip dish).
Cigarette cup was cut
from the deep-well
bottom of a champagne
bottle. Salad
bowl (opposite) was
made from a gallon
jug, which turned out
to be surprisingly
easy to work with.*

Cigarette Cup

**Contemporary
Salad Bowl**

Summer Tumblers

Desk Set

Individual soda bottles
(left) cut into attractive
coolers or juice glasses.
The dish holding paper
clips (above) was made from
the bottom of an amber
bottle for cooking oil. The
nipped-in base of an
imported beer bottle makes a
neat pencil jar, or a
nicely shaped cocktail glass.

Cocktail Glass

Cola Cooler

The Pepsi-Cola bottle (opposite)
was cut while still wearing its label,
since the score was made well
above the label. This bottle was
scored on a horizontal cutter and the

Candy Jar

Kitchen Canister

cut completed by the heat/chill
method, but required care so neither
flame or melting ice would spoil
the label. Canisters (above) were
cut from wine bottles. Cutting
cork disks for the covers was harder.

II

Here's How

Cutting bottles is like baking bread or making love; you can get the general method and basic principles by reading a book on the subject, but you really have to get the feel of it before you know what it's all about.

My first attempt at bottle cutting was a disaster. It might not seem possible to complicate a basically simple and workable process so that it goes thoroughly haywire, but I managed. The instructions included with my first cutting kit suggested that I start with something small—a nonreturnable soda bottle, for example—but since it also declared that the process was foolproof, I figured there was nothing to be gained by fooling around with mundane preliminaries and right off tackled a magnum champagne bottle I had saved from some forgotten celebration. Right there was mistake number one. I could have started with a beer

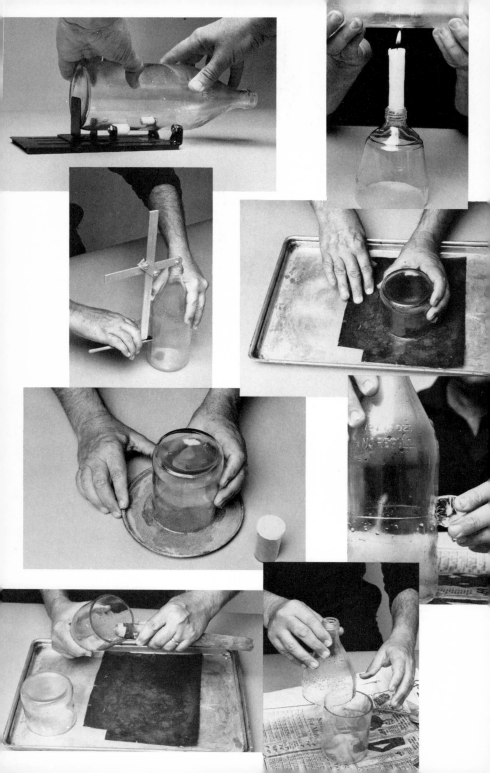

bottle, but in my eagerness to get going on something significant, I elected to take my first steps on a bottle in which the glass was exactly four times thicker. Now it isn't anywhere near four times harder to cut thicker glass. As a matter of fact, contradictory as it might seem, thicker glass usually will cut better. But it does take a bit longer to do successfully. And it takes practice. And since the seam or mold marks on a bottle of thicker glass are apt to be significantly more prominent than on a bantam-weight, it is no way to begin. After all, you wouldn't ski Suicide Run your first time on the slopes, would you?

There is a famous story about a mythical Texan of incredible wealth who, unable to secure tickets for a concert that he wanted to attend at New York's Carnegie Hall, wired his East Coast representative to buy the entire block in which the concert hall was located. As soon as the deal was closed, the millionaire, eager to see his new property, chartered a plane to take him to New York, and a helicopter to fly him to the mid-town terminal. But once on the ground, he was unable to hire a cab. So, the weather being unusually fine, he decided that he would walk. There was only one problem—he hadn't the faintest idea which way to go. As luck would have it, he saw in the crowd a frail, elderly man wearing a tattered tailcoat and carrying a battered violin case. "Excuse me, sir," the Texan said to the forlorn-looking passerby who was even then on his way into a pawn shop to try to raise a few dollars on his violin, "but would you tell me how to get to Carnegie Hall?" The old man sighed, gave a wistful smile and said, "Practice. It's the only way. Practice. Practice. Practice."

It works with bottle cutting, too.

CUTTING TOOLS

Your largest financial investment in hours of fascinating, creative enjoyment probably will be the price of your bottle-cutting apparatus. Depending upon which kit you purchase and where you buy it, the cost might be anywhere from four to twelve dollars. Kits in the ten-dollar bracket are, by far, the most common.

Take time to do a little comparison shopping. One kit selling for $10.95 is superior in exactly one respect to a kit nationally sold at $8.95 through department, gift and hobby stores. For two dollars less, you get a somewhat terse set of instructions that must have been written by a graduate of the Western Union school of communications and a slightly more generous supply of sandpaper. The instruction booklet that accompanies the higher-priced kit features a lot of words printed in full caps FOR EMPHASIS, which becomes pretty emphatic at times, and admits that the kit is not too successful when it comes to cutting square, flat and other not-round bottles, although it goes on to detail how one might try to accomplish same. In truth, such shapes are highly unsatisfactory for cutting with the kits now on the market. Given half a chance on a cuttable bottle, the kits work amazingly well; trying to use them for purposes for which they are not well suited is like trying to teach a sparrow to talk—you might eventually be able to do it, but think how much more you could have accomplished with a parrot!

Various differences in terminology and packaging aside, there are only two basic types of bottle-cutting kits now being sold. To distinguish between them, I call one "horizontal," the other "vertical."

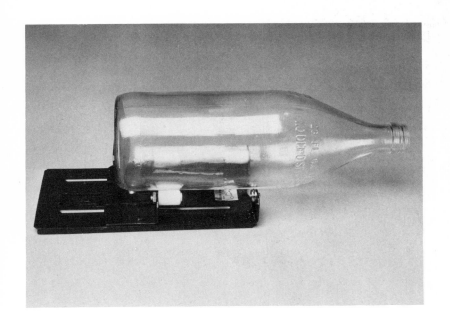

The Horizontal Bottle Cutter

With a horizontal kit, the bottle rests horizontally on a set of rollers attached to a metal base. The cutter wheel remains fixed while the bottle is revolved against it. When the bottle has been scored, the cut is completed by alternately heating and chilling the etched line.

The horizontal cutter can be used to score bottles and jars having cut-off or broken necks, or mouths too wide or too small to accommodate vertical cutting attachments, and it is, for the most part, easier to use for scoring bottles of standard sizes and shapes. Since the design of the horizontal cutter permits you to use both hands for turning the bottle, a smooth, even, consecutive score is easily achieved after a bit of practice.

The Vertical Bottle Cutter

The vertical cutting kits all work on pretty much the same principle—an ordinary glass cutter such as you might buy for one dollar at any hardware store is held in position by an adjustable metal bar, which once fixed at a point of the bottle, permits the cutter to score the glass while minimizing the usual this-way/that-way nonsense that otherwise might be caused by nerves, insecurity, faulty vision and, as Hamlet says, "the thousand natural shocks that flesh is heir to." The fracture line then is urged to complete cleavage by a series of snappy taps that accent and capitalize on its weakness, or the tapping apparatus can be ignored and the cut completed by temperature shock as it is with the horizontal kit.

Depending upon what you want to cut and how you want to cut it, there are advantages to each type of kit. The horizontal kit works perfectly well for bottles that would be uncuttable with a vertical cutter. There are, on the other hand, certain shapes and sizes that are much more successfully scored with the vertical kit. The tapping mechanism used to complete cuts made with the vertical kits is effective in most instances and fun to use once you have mastered the technique and made the essential and precise adjustments necessary for success. On the other hand, the heat-chill method used with the horizontal cutting technique is frequently faster and easier, requires no elaborate setting of equipment, and usually results in a cleaner break. Ideally the "compleat" bottle cutter would avail himself of the best features of both types of kits by acquiring one of each. If interest, ambition or curiosity seems insufficient to impel you to go quite that far, rest assured that with a bit of practice and careful attention to the instructions that will accompany your kit, you can have every expectation of success with either type. In many instances the choice will resolve itself on the basis of which type of bottle cutter one first happens upon when he sets out to buy one.

Bottle-cutting kits usually can be purchased at variety stores, hobby shops, gift shops, even book stores and stationers having craft and toy departments. This is not to suggest that the bottle-cutting equipment should properly be classified as a toy—one manufacturer refers to his product as a "precision tool," and he is not greatly exaggerating—but only that merchandise categories are apt to be fairly general and somewhat capricious.

Various craft houses and merchandise services will fill your mail orders for bottle-cutting kits. Specifications, prices, shipping and handling charges vary considerably and should be checked in advance.

Cut Clean

Start with a clean bottle from which you have removed all labels, foil, metal caps, strips, bands and any lumps of glue that were holding same. No matter which type of cutter you are using, you will have to remove the bottle's stopper, cork or cap. This is *essential,* so you might as well do it right away. (See Chapter Five: "The Bottle Washer's Guide.")

Assemble Cutter

It is a good idea to unpack the kit one element at a time and, insofar as possible, to assemble the various parts as you go. Simultaneously unwrapping all the bars and nuts and washers of a vertical cutter can be very confusing when it is time to tell washer A from washer B and one wing nut from another. Some parts might be perfectly interchangeable, others not, even though they might appear to be identical. Whatever you do, don't lose any of the little washers, screws and nuts that come with your kit, because if you have to go searching for replacements you could wind up having to buy another complete kit in order to obtain them.

Variations of one sort or another have been worked on the basic vertical kit by various companies; some have simplified their designs, others have made them more elaborate. One of the most recent vertical arrivals on the market features a cork-shaped cone that fits into the mouth of the bottle and keeps the cutter-holder from riding around, which strikes me as a step in the right direction, but the vertical kits that do not include this interesting feature also work perfectly well. My horizontal cutter kit came preassembled, leaving me nothing to do but read through the simple, well-expressed instructions for use.

It is impossible to give assembly directions that would apply across the board to whatever kit you happen to be using. There will be—or there *should* be; write to the manufacturer if there isn't—a set of instructions included in your kit. *Read them carefully and follow them exactly.* Don't worry if some of the hieroglyphics seem incomprehensible at first. Take the assemblage process one step at a time and gradually they will become crystal clear. And if they don't, and you have incorrectly positioned a disk or reversed a bent washer, you'll find out fast enough as soon as you start scoring or tapping.

One general guideline: Be sure that the cutting instrument is held securely. Of course, if you set every nut dead tight, you may have to reach for the pliers each time you want to alter some alignment. A drop of oil on the bolts will help keep things adjustable. It takes a bit of time to loosen things between cuts, but it sure beats winding up with a bunch of imperfectly scored bottles.

Work Wet

Before beginning to cut your first bottle, cover the table or counter top or wherever you are going to be working with a generous pad of damp newspaper. If you have acquired a jelly-roll pan or similarly suitable shallow tray in which you plan to work, you can run a bit of water into it and then line it with several thicknesses of newspaper. The paper gradually will absorb the water and your work surface will be suitably moist. After you have made a couple of passes with the bottle cutter, you will find that the wet paper is curdling into unattractive little lumps and smears, at which point it will be necessary to gather up at least the several top layers and replace them with fresh newspaper.

Working on damp newspaper has several advantages in bottle cutting. For one thing, your bottle is much less likely to slip while you are working with it than it would be on a smooth, dry surface. Additionally, any small splinters of glass or particles of glass dust that you happen to dig out in scoring a bottle or tapping-off a cut will tend to hold to the wet paper instead of dancing off in the next breath, and, accordingly, can be more neatly disposed of.

You might not realize it, but the glass cutter, for all that it *seems* not to be doing much, is grinding out minute particles of glass as the bottle is turned past it. In addition, stray flakes and shavings and needle-sharp shards are apt to break off as the cutting operation is completed. So why not have them all together, trapped on damp newspaper and confined within your jelly-roll pan? It makes bottle cutting just that much safer and makes cleanup a downright breeze.

You'll want to work wet when finishing the edges of your cut bottles, too, but that satisfying moment comes a bit later.

Lubricate Lightly

Put a drop of oil on the cutter wheel. Now! Before you try to cut anything. And before you forget. Oil the cutter wheel again when you have finished scoring your first bottle. And get in the habit of oiling the wheel again after every cut.

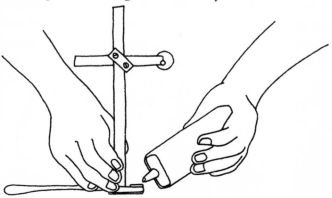

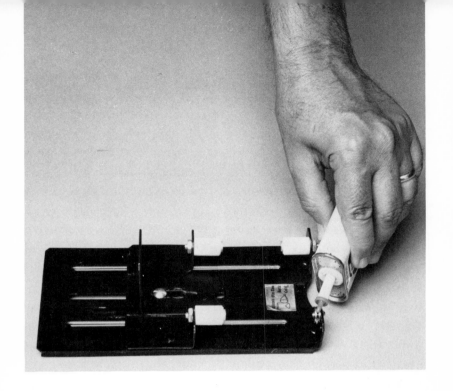

Protect Your Eyes

Hold on a minute! What about your eyes? If you aren't already wearing glasses, maybe this would be a good time to go get them, or whatever it is that you plan to use to protect your eyes. Yes, bottle cutting is safe, and yes, you must wear something to shield your eyes. Don't be balky about it—put them on. Keep them on until you have finished sanding smooth the edges of whatever it is you've cut the bottle into. If you feel awkward wearing glasses or goggles, think how much more awkward you would feel with glass dust or sandpaper scrapings irritating those big baby-blues.

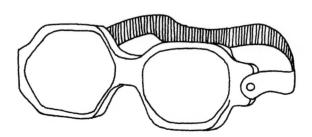

Score Softly

This is not precisely the moment of truth, but it is the one without which that moment simply cannot occur. What you want to do is have the cutter blade make a single clean continuous score around the bottle at the point at which you want the glass to separate.

So first you have to determine that point. If you are using a vertical-type kit, you adjust the cutter holder so that the blade is at a *clean right angle* to the surface of the bottle at that point. This is one of the most important adjustments that you must make. The degree of accuracy with which you accomplish it will greatly control the cleanness with which your bottle will divide. If the blade is not in perfect alignment to the bottle, the line that you score will be wider than it should be and the ultimate break will tend to be rough and irregular.

If you are using a horizontal-type cutter, you simply place the bottle on the cradle, positioning the bottle so that the cutter wheel lies under the point at which you want the bottle to separate, and adjust the back stop and the rear rollers accordingly. When that adjustment has been made, the screw that holds the back stop in place is tightened and the cutter is ready to use.

With either type of cutter, applying too much pressure when scoring the bottle will result in an irregular break. What you are using is a bottle cutter, you know, not a bulldozer. Pressing too hard gets into the "excess syndrome" to which many of us fall victim. One nice clean little line, fine as a hair and no deeper than a breath, will usually produce a crisp, even edge when the cut is completed.

I have learned that the best cuts, like some of life's best moments, are the quiet ones. What you want to do is to pass the

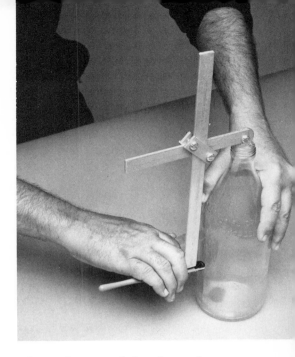

cutter blade *once* smoothly and evenly around the circumference of the bottle. If any sound accompanies this, it should be a faint whisper that hints of success and not a great groan of pending disappointment. The bottle-cutting instruction manuals that I have read give emphasis to this point, but one of the cautions they generally fail to cite is that pressing the bottle too hard against the cutter blade not only will result in irregular edges, but actually can gouge out splinters of glass that are, at best, a nuisance. So for the sake of your fingertips as well as the edges of your bottles, let discretion be your watchword. Score softly, and with a light hand. The bottle cutter will do the work, all you need to do is serve as its gentle guide.

With the vertical-type cutter, once you have it in proper alignment to the bottle and have secured all adjustable parts so that nothing is going to slip out of alignment as you work, with your left hand *slowly and smoothly* rotate the bottle in a *counterclockwise* direction while steadying the cutter with your right hand.

You want to press the cutter *gently* against the bottle as the bottle turns against it.

Ideally, you would complete one continuous revolution of the bottle while exercising steady pressure with the cutter, and your bottle would be scored with an even, unbroken line that ended smack on the spot where it started. Sounds simple, doesn't it? All you have to do is not stop turning the bottle with one hand while exercising absolute and unvarying control with the other. It isn't as bad as trying to rub your head while patting your stomach, but it isn't as easy as it sounds, either—largely because you cannot complete a full rotation of the bottle without, at some point along the way, altering your grip on it. Go ahead, try. Write if you find a way. At one point, I thought it might be efficient to set the bottle on a turntable—a lazy Susan seemed like a right-enough solution—and smoothly rotate it on that. Trouble was that while the bottle revolved as it should, so did my bottle-mounted vertical cutter-holder, unless substantial pressure was applied against it. That resulted in exactly the kind of deep and uneven score that I was trying to avoid. I suppose a satisfactory turning apparatus could be rigged up, but with a little practice and a modicum of

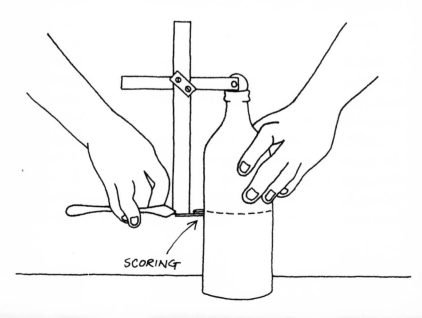

SCORING

manual dexterity, you should be able to achieve a perfectly dandy result turning the bottle by hand. Try to score at least half the bottle's circumference in one unbroken turn. Do the other half in a second. If that seems awkward, settle for the longest turn you can comfortably accomplish and remember that smooth, even pressure with the cutter is more important to success than the ability to snake your wrist around in a single full revolution of the bottle.

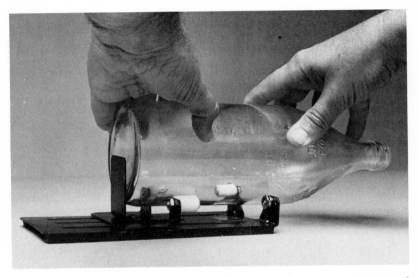

It takes from ten to fifteen seconds to complete one full turn of an average bottle. Still, you have to contend with that instant when your concentration was interfered with and your score interrupted sufficiently to leave a tiny gap or two somewhere along the way. There's nothing for it but to go back and fill in the blanks, being extremely careful not to overcut previously scored places. This is a tricky business and, quite honestly, is hardly worth the effort. Unless you happen to be working on a very special bottle that you are disinclined to abandon, it might be best to skip the

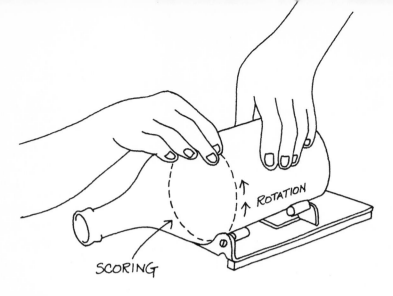

ROTATION

SCORING

whole process and start with a clean slate and a new bottle.

If your bottle cutter is the horizontal type, you simply lay the bottle lengthwise on the cutter, aligning the point at which you want the bottle to separate with the cutter wheel. Then bring the adjustable back stop up against the bottom of the bottle and secure it in place by tightening the screw that holds it and the rear set of rollers in position.

The bottle is slowly and gently rotated *toward* you. As you turn it, you apply steady, even pressure to produce a light score. Since this cutter allows you to have both hands available for rotating the bottle, you should be able to complete a single continuous score without interruption. As with the vertical cutter, only one revolution of the bottle is needed—or desired.

With either cutter you will hear a harsh grating sound when the cutting wheel has returned to the start of the score. What you hear is the blade scratching and scraping as it grinds away at the gritty glass that is grinding right back at it. So stop already! If you continue, you'll only succeed in damaging the cutter blade and ruining what otherwise might have been a very neatly etched line.

Check Continuity

Detach the cutting apparatus from the bottle, or remove the bottle from its cutting cradle, and get to know the score. Does it start and finish in one continuous line? Or does it look the way cantaloupes always look when I try to halve them neatly and somehow never wind up with the knife less than one-quarter inch out of alignment? You can fool around with a cantaloupe—cut a bit out here, level off a hill there; even give up on halves and divide the melon into wedges. With a bottle that you want to cut, however, *a noncontinuous score is uncuttable.* Forgivable, yes. Finishable, no. If you find that you have a tendency for misalignment, check to see that the various adjustable elements have been securely tightened. And that you aren't pressing too hard on the cutter bar if you are using a vertical cutter. Irregular pressure can produce the same result with a horizontal cutter, although a noncontinuous score is easier to avoid with that type.

Eventually—and sooner rather than later—everyone winds up with an imperfect score. There's nothing for it but to chuck the bottle, unless you want to salvage it by making a fresh score elsewhere on the bottle, where the glass remaining above or below the original line can be made use of. It is a good idea not to try to complete the cut of a scored line that is less than one inch from another. Zigzag cracks are likely to branch out between the two stress points and you'll wind up with a bottle having lots of interesting interior flaws and not too much serviceability.

Managing Multiples

Subject, however, to the one-inch limitation, you can continue making multiple cuts in a bottle as long as you remember to cut always from the bottom up if you are using a top-attaching cutting device. You can cut from the top down if you are using a horizontal cutter.

Suppose you wanted to cut the bottom of a bottle to use as an ashtray, and then you thought it would be nice to cut from the middle a few circles to be used as curtain rings, and that the neck and shoulder of the bottle would work well as a hanging planter. If you measure down from the top to the point at which you think you would like to make your planter cut, score it and remove it, you've had it with that bottle as far as the vertical cutter is concerned. You have your planter element and a cylinder of glass that might make a perfectly fine vase or tumbler or whatever, but you are not going to be able to accomplish any more cuts in the lower portion of the bottle for the excellent reason that you have removed the mouth of the bottle, which you need to hold your vertical cutter. You could, of course, continue making cuts up the top portion of the bottle, as long as it remained of sufficient length to permit use of the cutter holder. Unless the cut edge has been finished perfectly smooth, however, you might find it difficult to turn the remaining portion so that the next score will be even and effective. But let's face it, if you took the top off first, and you are using a vertical-type bottle cutter, you never will wind up with that ashtray.

Now on the other hand, if you start at the bottom with your vertical cutter, and score the line at which you would like the bottle to break for the ashtray, you either can continue to score the other cuts that you plan, or stop, cut off the bottom, sand smooth the rough bottom edge of your now-open bottle, reset your cutter at the next point and proceed as if you were working on a complete bottle. Again, be sure that the cut edge is absolutely smooth and even or you will have trouble turning the bottle against the cutter wheel.

I think it's a good idea to complete each cut before scoring the next. For one thing, it avoids the risk of stress cracks—except, of course, for those that might have resulted from imperfections in the glass, or in your tapping-off technique. For another, in case anything does go wrong, you haven't wasted time scoring for cuts that you won't be completing. Makes sense, don't you think? In favor of scoring all projected cuts, and then completing them from the bottom up, is the fact that a complete bottle is somewhat easier to turn than one from which the bottom has been removed.

If you are using a cutter of the horizontal type, you can cut from the top down or from the bottom up, although the former seems to produce a smoother result, largely because the bottle bottom remains to rest against the back stop and consequently the bottle usually can be revolved more smoothly than it otherwise might. There's a subtle benefit in balance, too, probably because of the slight additional weight that the bottle bottom provides. It is possible with a horizontal cutter to make a second or even a seventeenth cut in a bottle from which the bottom has been removed. It just seems slightly easier to me, when working with this cutter, to score multiple cuts from the top down, saving the cut nearest the bottle bottom for the last.

A multiple cut of a different kind will confront you for some projects—the need to cut several bottles to identical specifications. The most practical way to manage this is to line up all the bottles you plan to use, set your cutting apparatus and score each bottle in succession without having to stop to reset the cutter. Then you can complete the breaks on the same assembly-line basis. It's a good idea to score a few bottles more than you actually plan to use. Saves time and trouble in case anything goes wrong when it's finishing time.

Shine a Little Light on the Subject

You will find it a great convenience and a distinct help in completing the cutting operation to work where an overhead light or a table lamp can shine *through* the bottle as you work on it. If the light were the sun and you were the earth, the bottle should be pretty much where the moon would be at time of full solar eclipse. This point in the procedure is a good one at which to switch on the light.

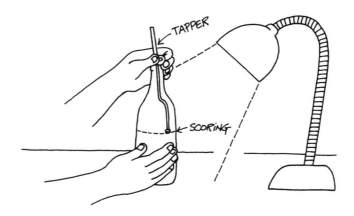

Completing the Cut

Most bottle-cutting sets operate on the simple principle that under stress glass will fracture at its weakest point. What you have done by scoring the bottle with the glass cutter is to create a convenient point of weakness at which the glass will oblige you by breaking. What you are going to do to complete the cut either with the tapping mechanism or through temperature shock is to capitalize on that weakness and encourage the glass to do what comes naturally, and to do it in a neat, orderly and prompt fashion.

If you are going to use tapper action for this purpose, then the second most important adjustment that you must make is to bring the tapper mechanism into perfect alignment with the cutting score. This would be a very easy thing to do if you had about five hands. Happily, it is not at all impossible to accomplish with two—merely tricky. And this is the reason for starting with clean bottles. Because if your bottle is less than sparkling clear, how do you suppose you are going to see whether or not your tapper really is tapping precisely where it ought to? As far as I know, there's only one way to tell, and that is to look through one side of the bottle to see that the tapper is connecting exactly on the line at the opposite side. Working with a good overhead light on the opposite side of the bottle will help enormously, but only if you also are working with a clean bottle. So aren't you glad that you did such a terrific job of washing up?

Insert the tapper into the bottle, and try for an approximate alignment. Then hold the tapper so that it touches the inner surface of the bottle directly opposite you, and bring it precisely onto the line. *Precisely.* You are not going to get anything but a junior version of the "Anvil Chorus" and maybe a sore thumb and possibly a cracked bottle if you fail to position the tapper accurately. It isn't all that hard, but it's important. You probably can break the bottle (break, that is, in the desired sense of the word) if you tap a breath above or below the line, but your break is not going to be clean and you're going to spend an awful lot of time pinging away with the tapper.

You must have the tapper in perfect alignment with the score on the side opposite you and tap *always away from yourself.* (Away, for that matter, from anyone else who might be kibitzing while you cut, too.) I never have had a bottle shatter during the tapping process, but there could be a first time, and there *are* those tiny fragments of glass left behind by the cutter wheel.

Since you will be working the tapper in that direction, it is essential that the exact alignment be made in that position. Never mind that it looks as if it would work equally well to adjust the tapper to the scored line as you face it, even though you would be tapping in the opposite direction. Believe me, it doesn't work.

Once you have the tapper set and the position fixed and secured, you can check the alignment by holding the bottom of the bottle against your chest and the tapper against the inner surface at what would be the North Pole if the bottle were the earth and the scored line were 0 degrees longitude.

Now, with the tapper in proper position, return the bottle to your damp-newspaper-lined tray, and remembering to tap away from yourself, give a light but definite forward swing to the tapper. Turn the bottle slightly and give another. And another, after the next slight turn. Continue to turn the bottle as you tap smartly at the interior exactly opposite the scored cutter line.

Having a light above and just beyond the bottle will help enormously as you continue tapping off, because as the tapper action actually breaks the glass, the light will reflect brilliantly along the line of fracture. You actually will be able to see the difference.

You will hear the difference, too. There is a distinct change in the sound made by the glass where the cut has been completed. You could chart your progress by ear as well as by eye. When you first begin, the sound of the tapper action is only a monotonous kind of "ping-ping-ping" as metal strikes glass. Once you have succeeded in breaking through to the outer surface, the "ping" kind of flattens out into "pang," as you tap that point on the bottle. When it does, you can ease the break forward by tapping lightly at either side of it, using the light-line as your guide.

When the bottle has been completely cut through, the tapper action will produce a dull sound that practically articulates the word "crack!" You'll recognize it when you hear it. And you will note that the band of bright light that reflects in the break completely encircles the bottle.

At that point, don't be surprised if the top cut portion practically leaps off the bottle. No, it isn't going to fly away, it's just celebrating its first shock of liberation. It doesn't happen every time, but it's an interesting effect and fun to behold.

On the other hand, you could encounter a bottle that, for one reason or another, just refuses to break clean at the cut line. It might break into insolent cracks along a mold seam, where the glass is slightly thicker and where the action of the cutter blade might have gotten imperceptibly out of alignment, or been otherwise imperfect. It might crack into crescents and curlicues as its fractures trace the stress spots caused by an impressed pattern or raised design. You might be able to finish the bottle if cracks radiate from the cutting score in one direction only. Tap carefully as you work your way around the bad spot, more or less as if you were trying to tiptoe past a squeaking floor board.

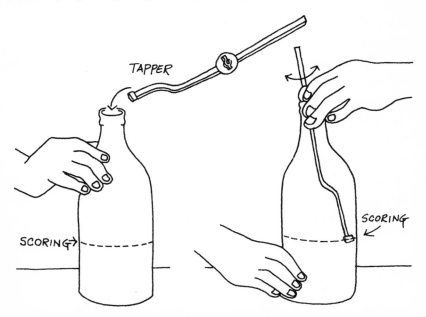

If the bottle is not developing interior cracks and your tapper is properly aligned and the cutting score is crisp and complete, maybe you simply are faced with a thick spot that needs extra care and attention. The thickness of the glass in many commercial bottles varies greatly—perhaps as much as a sixteenth of an inch. Keep cool and keep tapping. All other things being equal, success is yours, momentarily. Eventually you will be rewarded with that final "crack" sound that is the last sweet note in the bottle-cutter's concerto.

It takes a bit of practice to develop efficient tapper action. Whatever you do, don't clang the tapping rod back and forth as if you were ringing a bell. The action of the tapper should be smooth, crisp. The contact definite. Don't charge at the glass as if you were hurling a wrecking ball at the side of an old brownstone. Start each tap from about the center of the bottle and deliver a nice snappy tap. Give the bottle a slight turn and deliver another smart tap right on target. That's really all there is to it. Listen to the sound of the bottle as it begins to break, and watch the brilliant line of light spread as the break widens. Keep tapping away and before you know it your bottle will be cut and ready for finishing.

Fire and Ice

A different method for completing the break you have scored with your cutter wheel is to shock the glass into separating along the etched line through alternating applications of heat and cold. For my money, this technique has tapping off beat all to blazes. It is the only method recommended by the distributors of the horizontal bottle cutters. Happily, it can be used successfully to complete any cut—all other things being equal. You can, in fact, use the fire-and-ice technique to separate bottles that would otherwise be uncuttable. I even have used it in cutting flat glass surfaces. And not only does the heat-cold method succeed with bottle shapes that would not permit completion by tapping off, but it also works much faster. Plus which, you are saved the tricky business of setting the tapper so that it precisely connects with the glass at the etched line, and keeping it on target until the bottle has been completed. And I, for one, think the fire-and-ice system results in a smoother edge than even the most meticulous tapping off can produce. Of course the edges still must be polished and sanded smooth, but the cleaner the break, the less trouble you are going to have bringing it to perfection.

AN IMPORTANT CAUTION: *Before you begin this process, remember that the bottle must be open at one end before it is heated.* Otherwise the expanding warm air trapped in the bottle could cause it to explode. (Nasty business and certainly to be avoided!) Just be sure the cork is out, the stopper removed, or the cap off, unless, of course, you previously had cut open the bottom. If you haven't, and you don't, blame yourself if Mother Nature does it for you. And she won't be around to pick up the pieces, either!

What you do, simply, is to heat the bottle along the etched line, by holding the bottle horizontally, so that the cutter score is just a breath above the tip of a candle flame, and slowly turn the bottle a few times. Rotate the bottle slowly at first, turning it over and over in one direction and keeping the etched line just above the flame. When you have completed a few revolutions, the glass probably will begin to feel warm, and you can turn the bottle a bit more rapidly through another three or four quick rotations in order to spread the heat more evenly along the cutter score.

Do not hold the bottle *in* the candle flame. That will help nothing. It also probably will produce an annoying band of smoky

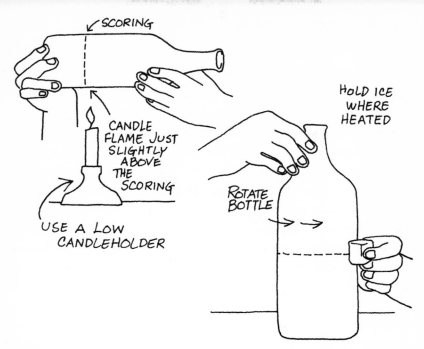

SCORING

CANDLE FLAME JUST SLIGHTLY ABOVE THE SCORING

USE A LOW CANDLEHOLDER

HOLD ICE WHERE HEATED

ROTATE BOTTLE

smudge that tends to obscure the etched line. It also tends to warm a wider area of glass than you either need or want to have heated, which can result in unwanted cracking along the line of separation when the glass is cooled.

After the scored line has been heated, set the bottle upright and immediately pass an ice cube along the mark. You will be able to see the crack develop as the ice is moved down the line—unless, of course, you have smudged things up by holding the bottle too near the candle flame. When you have passed the ice once around the bottle, check the light reflection along the line to see that the crack is complete. It is a good idea to hold both parts of the bottle to be sure that one section does not drop off and break. One set of instructions suggests giving the bottle a slight tug to encourage the two parts to separate, although urging you not to try to "force them apart." Usually you will need not even a slight tug. When the break is complete, the bottle will separate. If it does not, check it in the light and you probably will

see where the crack has not gone completely through the glass.

You might feel that this procedure is too simple to be effective. Until, that is, you give it a try. Simple it is. Effective, too.

If you do not succeed in separating the bottle after a single heat-cold attempt, wipe the bottle dry and repeat the heating process, being careful to hold the bottle at both sides so that if the cut is suddenly completed during this reheating process, you do not risk having one part break away. Should the break not be completed during the second heating, again upend the bottle, and holding the top part, apply ice again to the heated score.

You can repeat the heating and chilling process several times if it seems necessary. In most cases, if you have properly heated the bottle, you will need to attempt it only once. Naturally, it takes longer to alter the temperature of very heavy (thick) glass, and you might find that your dense-walled champagne bottles require a series of heat-cold treatments. However many they take, they probably will be completed more quickly than if you tried to tap them off. And when they do separate, they probably will break much more cleanly.

Whether heating or chilling, try to concentrate the temperature shock at the scored line. Hold an edge of the ice cube to the bottle precisely at the line instead of smearing it flat against both sides of the score. Play the tip of the candle flame just at the etched line, so that the warmth is concentrated there.

Again: Remember that the bottle *must* be open before you heat it. Probably you removed the cork, cap and all that nonsense back when you washed the bottle. If you didn't, do it before you hold the bottle over a candle or else risk having your bottle shatter.

The fire-and-ice method of completing the bottle cut is much more efficient than the tapping-off technique, which works perfectly well for some bottles, not at all for others. Even if you use a vertical-type cutter for scoring your bottles, I recommend that you try completing the cut with this heat-cold technique, which is the process used in conjunction with the horizontal cutter.

If the heat-cold technique has a disadvantage, it is that occasionally a bottle develops tiny vertical cracks along the cut line after the cut has been completed. These post-cutting cracks most often occur at the rims of bowl-shaped pieces cut at their widest diameter, where, I suppose, the expansion-contraction effect of the heat-cold treatment causes greater stress in the glass. If one of your cut-bottle articles displays such a tendency, you might take some consolation from the fact that this kind of flaw is not unknown in some of the finest, most carefully made and most expensive art-glass works. Nearly every known example of Steuben's rare Mandarin Yellow glass, for instance, has cracked—some pieces so badly that they have required repairs.

Keep a cloth handy when completing cuts by the fire-and-ice method. You will need it for wiping away moisture from melting ice and particularly for drying a bottle between repeated heat-cold procedures. And have matches at your elbow, and ice cubes within reach. As in Chinese cooking, much of the success of this process depends upon having all in readiness before you begin, because once you get started you are going to want to go one-two-three through the procedures. And of course, your candle flame will do its work just that much better if you permit it to function away from drafts. Even if it doesn't blow out, a flickering flame does not give the steady, even warmth that you want for heating your bottle.

Sanding Smooth

It is all over then but the sanding. The samples of paper that probably came with your kit will see you through your first few bottles. But it is much easier to work with a larger sheet. Take the newspaper out of your jelly-roll pan and cover the bottom surface with water about one-eighth of an inch deep. Lay your finishing paper sandy side up in the water and *work wet throughout this step*. All you really have to do is rub the edges of your cut glass around and around on the sandpaper. Turning the glass in a circular motion will give you the smoothest and most uniform sanding action. Use the 80-grade paper first to grind off any troublesome rough spots. Then cut a strip of the 320-grade paper, and *wet it* before you wrap it around the length of broom handle that you have saved for this final touch. This will give you a nice, convenient-to-handle tool for polishing any troublesome edges and will leave your glass with a quite professional-looking velvety-finished rim. If you use only the 180-grade paper, you can complete both smoothing steps with it. Just cut off a narrow strip to give a final cleanup wrapped wet around your wooden core.

You could do all this in the kitchen sink, as one instruction booklet suggests—as long as you didn't mind how badly you scratched the sink. Much better to leave all those scars in the jelly-roll pan, *n'est ce pas?*

Now run a fingertip along the smooth-sanded rim of your glass. Surprised to see how finely you have finished it? You're ready for the big time now.

*See photos and diagrams
on following pages*

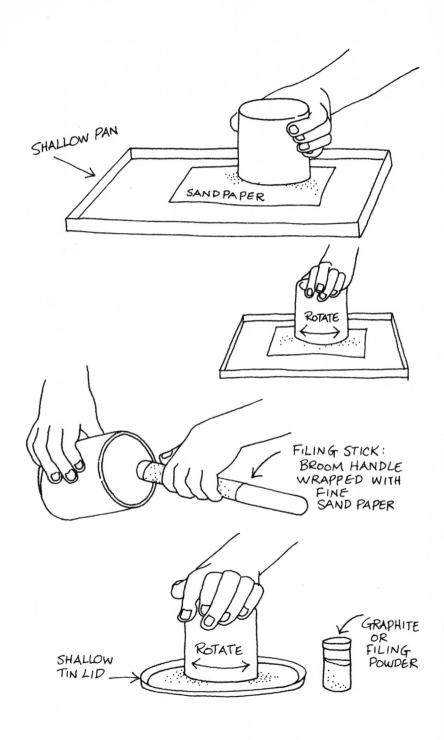

SHALLOW PAN

SANDPAPER

ROTATE

FILING STICK:
BROOM HANDLE
WRAPPED WITH
FINE
SAND PAPER

ROTATE

SHALLOW
TIN LID

GRAPHITE
OR
FILING
POWDER

Imported beer, gin and wine bottles offer interesting colors and shapes for some different and dramatic parfaits, vases, goblets and glasses. By epoxying bottoms to inverted tops, an astonishing variety of form and function is possible. Tall vase (opposite) was made from an Italian wine bottle, uncuttable by tapping off.

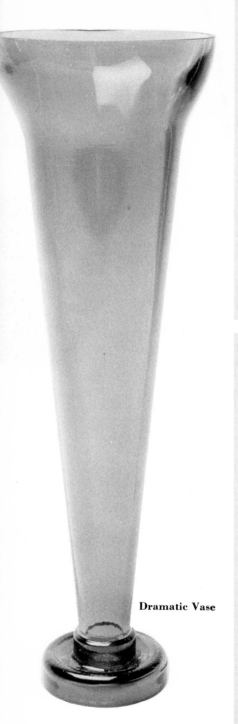

Dramatic Vase

Beer Goblet

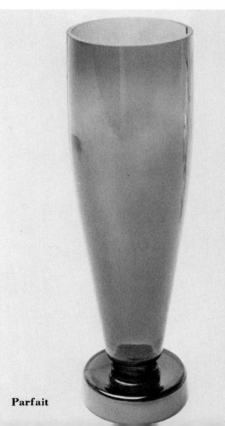

Parfait

Grissini Jar

*Bread sticks
in an upside-down
bottle that has
its neck under its
base (left).
Relish vase made
in same way
from gin bottle.*

Relish Vase

Slender Vase

Epergne

*Chianti bottle (left) is one
of the hardest to cut successfully,
but results justify the effort.
Mini-epergne (above) was cut from
a liqueur bottle, impossible
to complete through tapping off.*

After-dinner Fruit and Nuts

Modern Lighting

*Fruit bowl (opposite)
was cut from the top part
of a gallon wine jug;
its base is the inverted
bottom of a wine bottle.
The hanging triple lamp
(above) has shades cut
from three amber bottles
for cooking oil. A saucer
made from one of the cut-
off bottoms is pictured
on page 25. The open
canister is a quart
"No Return" club soda.*

What can you get in a wine bottle besides wine? A champagne glass, if you're clever, or a candy dish if you're willing to work out on a tricky bottle shape. The sleekly modern vase full of spring flowers (opposite), on the other hand, is a snap to redeem from a quart-size bottle for soda.

Champagne or Sherbet

Candy Dish

Clear Vase

III

Adhesives,
Accessories
and Additions

Soon after you have created a
few of the tumblers, vases, bowls and other more-or-less cylin-
drical objects that you can call forth simply by removing the top
or the bottom from a bottle, you undoubtedly will want to try
your hand at something a little more original and a little more
complex. And certainly you are going to want to try various
decorating and personalizing techniques that will make your
creations distinctively individual and add an element of color,
charm, perhaps even humor, or an extra dimension of utility.
At your local craft or hobby shop you will be dazzled by the
abundance awaiting you there. Not all decorating techniques are
suitable to glass, but many are, and with a little imagination, they
can help you turn the bottom of a bottle into a delightful little
party souvenir, or disguise the "No Deposit/No Return" legend
with a glittering fretwork of golden squiggles and swirls.

ON THE MATTER OF ADHESIVES

First, however, you probably are going to want to start joining bottle elements—attaching tops to bottoms, bottoms to tops and the like. There are a confusing number of adhesives on the market that will accomplish this feat for you. Some of the new silicone products are excellent and are highly recommended by craft instructors, but I think that clear epoxy can't be beat. One of the new quick-drying types really is first rate for use in cut-bottle projects. For one thing, it not only dries fast, but it also dries crystal clear, which is an advantage when working with a material of which clarity is a much-prized characteristic. Some of the silicone products harden to what I call tapioca gray, a slightly translucent, faintly visible texture that in some instances will make the glass look as if it were not quite clean. Not so the crystal-clear epoxies. (Some epoxy adhesives dry to an opaque-white porcelainlike finish. Blame yourself if you fail to read the label carefully.)

You'll find it easy to create artistic shapes if you epoxy parts of bottles together. Just a little dab of epoxy will be strong enough to support the heavier part of the bottle on the small diameter of the bottle neck.

The clear epoxies have the advantage of invisibility, in the event a surplus trickle happens to drip down inside one of your creations where it might be difficult or impossible to remove. And most importantly, properly prepared and applied, they will continue to hold together the elements they are supposed to hold together—presumably until doomsday, and certainly for as long as the glass itself survives.

If there is anything at all difficult about using these miracle new epoxies, it is finding a suitable surface on which to mix the twin elements of epoxy adhesive and hardener. I use large paper plates because they are cheap, convenient and disposable. The plates also are large enough to permit me to steady a plate with one hand while the other furiously stirs the two ingredients to the essential thorough blend, without making my thumb or my elbow part of the mixture. I use a small plastic picnic knife as a spatula, breaking out a fresh one for each new epoxy session. Probably I could reclaim the knife, but usually by the time I am ready to tidy up and put away, the knife has cemented itself to the plate. If it hasn't, I know that something was amiss in my epoxy mixture and that I probably will have to redo my glass project, starting with a fresh batch of adhesive. It's extravagant with picnic knives, but it makes a great test run for the epoxy.

For best results with the fast-setting epoxy, work with small batches, mixing only as much as you expect to use for each article, and putting it to work before it has too much time to start hardening. The only time one of my epoxied glass projects came apart was when I tried to use the last semisolid scrapings from an about-to-harden batch. It held for a while, but simply could not bond with the strength that would have developed from a freshly blended supply. You need not use a great amount of these miracle adhesives, since they hold equally well even in thin films.

If you have trouble making a particular connection hold, you might try to roughen the glass surface slightly with a few touches of your finishing paper. It is unlikely that you will need to resort to this, but keep it in mind, just in case. Makes a world of difference. Of course you'll roughen the glass where the frosted scratching will not show, won't you?

The cautions on my package of fast-setting epoxy state: "May cause skin irritation. Wash with soap and water. Do not take internally. Keep out of reach of children." All of which makes perfectly good sense, so pay attention. They don't put those warnings on products just to fill up space on the label, you know.

STAINED GLASS IN TWO STEPS AND TWO MINUTES

All right, so it isn't going to look like the real, genuine, furiously expensive Tiffany glass. The stained-glass effects that you create to decorate your cut-bottle articles are going to look quite different. That, however, doesn't mean they aren't going to be beautiful. Different, distinctive and absolutely enchanting. And what's more, they are a lot of fun to do. And easy! Your craft store will have, or will obtain for you, a terrific liquid stain that dries to brilliant transparent color and which is called, appropriately enough, "Glass Stain," that being exactly what it is. It is available in small jars—a little goes a long way—of individual color encompassing an astonishingly broad and beautiful spectrum. What's more, as if the jewellike tones of the stains were not in themselves overwhelming, you can mix and blend colors to produce an unlimited variety of shades and tones. And it flows like a dream.

Trouble is, particularly on a curved surface such as you probably are going to be decorating, it flows altogether too well, and unless you want to duplicate the effect of one of those flocculent, multicolor *pâte de verre* creations, you are going to have to erect some sort of wall to contain the stain. This, however, produces precisely the kind of "leaded" effect that suggests costly stained-glass productions.

There are several "liquid-lead" products on the market and some of them are very good. Some, on the other hand, simply leave your glass looking as if gray worms had expired upon it. One of the least expensive, easiest to use and most effective products suitable for "leading" your pieces of stained glass is sold in hardware stores under the name "Liquid Solder." It dries quickly to a silvery, pewterlike finish, although the package defines it as "nonmetallic." It flows on smoothly with about as much effort as you might need to press decorative cake frosting through a pastry tube, and it is, consequently, easy to control.

What you want to do is define each color segment of your design by outlining it in liquid solder. To put it more directly: you draw the picture in liquid solder, and when you have finished and the outlines are set, you color it with liquid glass stain. It is attractive to break the design up into small sections, which seems to

An old plant stand with a new paint job plus 8 candles in stain-decorated shades equals an unusual patio light.

accent the jewellike beauty of the glass stains. This has the advantage of making it easier to have the stain in each area consistently smooth, too.

Remember: Liquid solder is an extremely flammable substance and should be carefully used well away from fire or flame. There are warnings against excessive inhalation, prolonged contact with skin and eyes and internal ingestion.

It is easier to draw or paint on the glass if you hold it horizontally. If you have trouble drawing the design directly on the glass, try drawing it first with a black felt pen on a piece of plain white paper. Then snip out the design and hold it (you can fix it in place with a snip of transparent tape, if you want) inside the glass. You can follow along the lines as you apply the liquid solder to the outer surface. This is a good technique to use if you want to decorate several pieces with matching designs, or if you are trying to do something particularly complicated.

You can use the same trick to help you when you are ready to apply the colored stains, too. Do a colored example with felt pens or wax crayons on white paper, hold it inside the glass and use it as a color guide while you apply the appropriate glass stains to the surface. It makes sense and saves brush cleaning to do all the areas that are going to be one color while you work in that color. If your design is at all involved, it is easy to forget to fill in some fugitive area, and it's a nuisance to have to go back, so even if you don't trouble to use a color guide under the glass, it's a good idea to have a finished example in front of you for ready reference.

As applied in one thin coat, the glass stain colors may seem less rich and deep than you would like. A more intense color can be achieved by applying a second, third, seventeenth coat of stain, letting each dry completely before brushing on the next. You can also flow on a heavier coat of stain, using a saturated brush, but this usually results in uneven color, thick in some spots, thin in others, and puddling into moons along the lead dividers at the down-curve of the glass.

The glass stain also is a flammable mixture and should not be used anywhere near you-know-what. It is dangerous—perhaps fatal—if swallowed, and is irritating to skin and eyes. So use a brush, keep out of reach of the kids, and avoid excessive inhalation. And read and observe the cautions set forth on the bottle.

I have seen brown and green bottles treated with transparent colored stains, and to my mind, most of them fail pretty miserably. You can work out some interesting effects with the blue stains applied to green glass, and with the reds, oranges and red-browns applied to brown and amber. Pretty effects are possible with pale aqua glass, which lends itself to decoration with delicate tints. Best use of the transparent stains, however, is to decorate clear, colorless bottles that otherwise might be lacking in interest, and on which the lovely transparent colors can be appreciated in their full beauty.

A rich glass-mosaic look is achieved by artfully painting some areas with color upon color and by filling in adjacent areas with the individual stains. And there are opaque black and white stains available to add variety and contrast, or to be painted over with some of the transparent colors for even more varied work. The opaque colors work well on some of the darker glasses and add a striking contemporary note when combined with the soft gleam of the hardened liquid solder.

These permanent stains wear well. They are, however, less durable than fired-on colors and will not survive cleaning with harsh abrasives. This is also true of many commercial pieces treated with mineral stains, so *gentle* is the watchword. A quick swish in lukewarm water to which you have added a splash of detergent, followed by a tepid rinse in clear water ought to be sufficient and safe.

PRESERVING LABELS

Plastic spray can be used to coat a label that you want to preserve on a bottle. Children especially enjoy using tumblers cut from cola or soda bottles on which the label has been retained. This would seem to contradict the instruction that all labels, etc., be removed from any bottle that you plan to cut—which only goes to prove that to all rules there can be exceptions. You can carefully soak the label off, let it dry and paste it back on the bottle after it has been cut. Or you can cut the bottle where the label will not interfere with the scoring and finishing process, in which case, you can perfectly well leave it on. Of course if you are planning to save the label on a bottle that you want to cut with the fire-and-ice technique, be sure that you won't be cutting the bottle where the label might be scorched, smudged or ruined by ice-cube drippings. In which case it would be best to remove the

label before you start to cut the bottle, and to restore it after the cut has been completed.

Several light coats of plastic spray will give better protection than a single thick one. Some of the plastic coatings are more durable than others. To one degree or another all of them are washable, but you might not want to risk the plastic protection to the extreme temperatures of an automatic dishwasher.

PASTE-ONS FOR READY-MADE DECORATIONS

Decals, or "decorative transfers" if you want to get formal about them, can be fast friends for the bottle decorator. In a changing world there is something wonderfully comfortable about these familiar decorative techniques that work pretty much today as they worked when my great aunt used them to put pictures of vegetables, fruits and flowers on the painted doors of her kitchen cupboards. Today's decals are available in many varied designs from traditional Federal-type motifs (eagles, banners, drums) to flamboyant full-blown roses and charmingly styled nursery animals, and in many more functional forms (labels, name tags, initials) than my aunt would have dreamed of. And they seem to slip away from their backings more readily than they used to and to take hold somewhat more quickly. Or am I only more adroit than I was when I used to scissor out bunches of violently purple grapes and vividly orange carrots and faceless sunbonneted children to trim the kitchen woodwork?

In any event, the decals adhere perfectly well to glass and, artfully chosen, can make decorating and personalizing your bottle-cut articles a matter of instant achievement. Certainly there is no easier way to turn out a set of monogrammed glasses, or a uniformly labeled canister set. You can buy blank decal labels on

Inexpensive butterfly decals were used to decorate the top of a cut gallon wine jug. With a plant in the bottom part and the top replaced, you have a terrarium. Also an excellent miniature greenhouse for starting plants. Vertical cutter could score this type of bottle, but it cannot be completed by tapping-off process.

which you inscribe your own identifications, or preprinted labels for staples—flour, sugar, salt, rice—or for herbs, spices and just about anything else you might want to store and identify.

There's really no trick at all to applying decals to your glass articles. Follow directions for soaking the illustration away from its backing. Slide the design onto the glass, press out any wrinkles, working always from the center of the decal out to the edges— and there you are! You really can't go wrong. And if you subsequently decide that you did, you can eliminate a decal with the special remover sold for that purpose.

If you can't possibly find the decal design that you want (incredible though that seems) but you find exactly the illustration you want in a magazine, you can make your own decal by cutting out the picture and pasting it to the glass. Use a thin coat of white glue and be sure to carefully press out any wrinkles and to securely fix all edges. When the glue has hardened, you can preserve your decoration with a coat or two of clear plastic spray.

Bottle bottoms and circular sections make unusual, inexpensive Christmas favors, covered with "diamond dust" (from crafts shops) and miniature figures added for seasonal touch. Tiny plush leaves and clusters of glass beads were epoxied to wine bottle bottom (opposite page) to add a bit of sparkle.

PUT-ONS

Besides paper decals there are many attractive accessories that can be pasted onto your cut-bottle creations. In addition to the beads and flowers that you will find at your craft-supply shop, there are excellent decorative elements available from stores selling millinery supplies and similar trimmings. A friend of mine created some charming wall decorations by setting tiny bunches of bead flowers upon small round frames cut from bottle bottoms. Some were backed with circles of cardboard covered in silk moiré, others with metallic foil. With the addition of a bit of wire or a loop of pipe cleaner to serve as a hanger, these miniature still-lifes made a distinctive wall grouping.

PAINT-ONS

Acrylic paints in squeeze tubes and glittering, metallic-bright pastes that dry to permanent, sparkling bands of raised color are easy, inexpensive ways to add color and decorative brilliance to your glass creations.

Both work perfectly well with glass and make possible many interesting contrasts in texture and color. The metallic pastes are particularly useful for camouflaging undesirable legends in the glass ("No Deposit/No Return," f'rinstance) or for concealing unattractive joints where parts might have been more skillfully glued together.

The acrylic color choices include vibrant "Day-Glo" pinks and oranges. The glitter colors include a sparkling emerald green that is stunning when applied to similarly colored glass, plus red, silver, gold and a confettilike multicolor that would add a note of razzle-dazzle gaiety to any cocktail service.

With either paint or glitter, you will find that you work best if you hold the glass horizontally and if you keep the tube at a 45-degree angle to the surface. From time to time, you might find that the tube opening clogs and needs to be wiped cleaned with a bit of cloth, or perhaps reopened by inserting a pin. Use even, steady pressure and squeeze always, of course, from the bottom of the tube.

Be sure to observe any special cautions appropriate to these products. Some are highly flammable. Others warn against excessive inhalation. Working near an open window not only helps avoid that, it also encourages your decorations to dry more quickly.

*Shoulder and neck sections of soda
bottles epoxied for unusual shapes. Squiggles
of metallic paste cover "No Deposit . . ."
Midsection would make attractive tree ornament.*

CORK FOR STOPPERS, COVERS AND THE LIKE

Finding good cork is a problem. One craft-supply company, ever responsive to the needs of its market and aware of the growing popularity of bottle cutting, plans to introduce cork in solid sheets of suitable thickness for cutting into covers and stoppers. Until they do, you might consult your classified telephone directory for a possible source. I found mine listed under "Cork and Cork Products," and maybe you will, too. If you don't, ask if your library can supply the classified directory of a nearby city and see if that won't yield a source for the kind of cork you need.

Remember when you order that tiles formed from pressed cork chips do not cut into smooth, durable lids and stoppers, so don't buy trouble by investing in them. And if a wholesale dealer seems reluctant to honor your modest request and suggests that he cannot be troubled to fill small individual orders, ask him to refer you to one of his regular customers who might be willing, for a small handling charge, to add your requirements to his next delivery.

Draw a paper pattern carefully to get exact size of cork to fit canister. Then cut cork to size, using a sharp knife or single-edge razor blade.

HANDLES, FINIALS AND DECORATIVE KNOBS

Drawer pulls, doorknobs and similar accessories never designed for use on glass can make practical and handsome additions to your cut-bottle pieces. Your lumber yard, builders' supply store, hardware store and closet shop undoubtedly will inspire
you with a selection of handles, finials and other accessories that
can be epoxied to your glass creations to give an extra dimension
of use and decoration. I happen to like the texture contrast of
wood and metal used with glass, but interesting effects also can be
achieved with some of the porcelain and glass knobs and pulls.
There are some sparkling, multifaceted crystal knobs that I would
not recommend for this use, however, principally because their
brilliance might make the less-fine bottle glass look somewhat
poor relation by comparison. Additions of wood, metal or ce-
ramic, on the other hand, can complement the glass by giving
emphasis to its clarity.

If you have difficulty applying such elements because of slightly nonconforming shapes, you might try to attach them with tiny lumps of one of the silicone adhesives.

BASES, STANDS AND SUCH

There is at least one widely distributed wrought-iron candle holder that easily is transformed into a hurricane lamp with the addition of a cut-bottle shade. You probably can pick up one, or a pair, or a dozen for that matter, at your craft-supply shop. If not, try one of the ubiquitous candle shops that currently seem to be flourishing all over the place.

Metal, stone and wood lamp bases also make attractive and

practical stands or bases for glass vases and other decorative objects, and usually can easily be recalled to service as bases for cut-bottle lamps. If you happen not to have any old table lamps sitting around waiting to supply you with suitable parts, your electrical supply shop probably can come through with a handsome assortment in diverse sizes and designs and quite inexpensively. And of course, the old faithful craft shop usually can be counted on for some interesting and useful shapes in unfinished wood.

Unfinished wood bases could be oil-finished with a light coat of boiled linseed oil and turpentine mixture, or you could stain them with one of the many easily rubbed-on wood finishes, paint them satin smooth with one of the snappy spray enamels, or for an absolutely stunning effect, brush on a layer of gold lacquer, and when it has hardened, color over it with some of your transparent glass stains. Use the same liquid-solder technique previously detailed, or separate your color divisions with one of the gold or silver squeeze-on products. This last might seem to be gilding the lily, but it gives an astonishingly rich, jewellike effect that makes an ordinary wooden base look as if it were extravagantly enameled.

Handsome wooden bases also can be obtained from some of the import shops and gift shops or stores featuring Oriental handcrafts. With the addition of a cut-bottle dome, these make interesting and inexpensive display cases for small arrangements of dried flowers, for a collection of jewelry, pill boxes, miniatures, dolls, or just to house a handsome piece of silver that you enjoy having on display but don't enjoy polishing all the time. Authentic Victorian display domes of this type are almost ruinously expensive —when you can find one in an antiques shop. With a suitable wooden base, your bottle-cut dome is virtually free!

Make it with macramé—
see next page

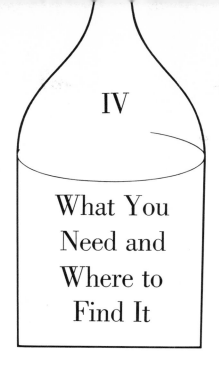

IV

What You
Need and
Where to
Find It

BOTTLES

O nce you really get involved in bottle cutting, you probably will find that the hardest part of your fascinating new hobby is obtaining an adequate supply of interesting cuttable bottles. Of course, you have your household empties to draw from, but very soon they can develop a certain uninspiring monotony as personal preferences and practicality contribute to a repeated pattern of brands and sizes.

An astonishing variety of color is available to the bottle cutter. One instantly thinks of clear (colorless) glass and the shade of green upon which bottles have bestowed a name, and the ubiquitous brown that would, at first wink, seem to round out a fairly limited palette. Untrue. Consider the bottles of rich royal blue and delicate aquamarine that line the grocer's and the pharmacist's shelves. Notice the lovely light green, or the peach tint of a

Rhine wine bottle, the smoky-yellow to gray-green of a French Sauternes or Chablis, the near-black of a noble Champagne, the pale but lively aqua that contains some Italian Chiantis, some domestic rosés. Observe the many shades—from golden honey to rich molasses—that are included in the generic, woefully unsuggestive designation: amber. And there are specialty bottles of frosted, translucent and opaque glass that further expand the spectrum of color and texture available to the bottle cutter.

To a great degree shape will dictate which bottle you will want to use for what project. But color and texture also are to be considered with regard to use. The shape of a clear glass jug might recommend it for cutting into a planter, but since there is nothing particularly attractive about drainage pebbles and dirt and tangles of planting fiber and root growth, one of the darker-colored glasses would be a better choice. Colorless bottles, on the other hand, would be preferred for cutting into wine glasses. Clear, or with the palest hint of aqua or green, would enhance but not obscure the beautiful color of the wine. And right as beer would seem in an amber tumbler, think how peculiar it would look served in a glass cut from a dark green wine bottle! Tomato juice, iced tea and coffee all look ill-at-ease in dark green glasses, which, however, do wonderful things for grapefruit juice, pineapple juice, lemonade, white-wine coolers, limeade and the like. Fortunately, bottle cutting is so easy and inexpensive that with a little ingenuity you can assemble complete sets of glasses in graduated sizes and as many attractive shapes and assorted colors as your bottle sources yield.

For variety, for speed, and for securing multiples of needed bottles, the serious bottle cutter soon will want to acquire bottles especially for cutting. This introduces two problems. The first is which bottles will and which will not prove satisfactory for cutting. The second problem is acquiring a sufficient supply of those that will.

Introducing the Uncuttables

The instructions that came with my first bottle-cutting kit said that I was equipped to cut any round bottle into a tumbler, or whatever else my fancy might suggest it be turned into. But I had a lot to learn, because let's face it, some bottles are distinctly uncuttable, and others are uncuttable with one kit although perfectly satisfactory if another is used.

If you are using a bottle-cutting set that requires "tapping off," for instance, there are bottle shapes that can make that essential step impossible. The how-to of tapping off is fully discussed in Chapter Two, but for purposes of bottle-selection or elimination it is necessary to know that tapping off is done with a metal wand tipped with a weighted washer which is inserted into the bottle. After the washer is brought into alignment with the line scored by the glass cutter, the action of the tapper—a swinging, back-and-forth movement—accents the fracture and completes the cut. The movement of the tapper might be compared to one-half the action of a bell clapper. And clapper or tapper, either needs some unobstructed room in which to swing, and isn't going to do any business unless it connects with the right part of the bell or bottle. A long, narrow neck on a bottle sometimes prohibits tapper action. So can a bottle with a seemingly acceptable neck, but having a sharply swelling bowl to which the tapper cannot reach. There is a method for completing these cuts, the fire-and-ice method, but tapping off is not part of it.

For cutting purposes, a useful bottle must be round. At least it must be round at the point at which it is to be cut. A flat area reserved for a label, for example, might not interfere with a successful cut as long as the bottle is perfectly round above or below that area. An oval, square, rectangular, triangular or other interesting bottle shape, however, belongs in the uncuttable category unless the bottle can be cut at some point on a round shoulder or base. Frequently it can.

Decorations, designs, patterns and lettering can render a bottle uncuttable if they permit no clear pass for the cutting blade. It is sometimes possible to score such a seemingly unusable bottle by carefully aligning the cutter between patterned rows as long as the design is sufficiently spaced to permit the cutting device to do its thing.

There is no need to reject a bottle of heavy, thick glass. Champagne bottles, for instance, are made extra strong in order to withstand the pressure of all those delightful little bubbles that make the festive wine so special. And, of course, the walls of a great magnum bottle are somewhat thicker than those of its dense little nieces and nephews. Yet magnum champagnes can be cut like a charm while many skinny little pushovers in the soda-and-beer divisions will display nasty tendencies to fracture, particularly along the mold seams.

Also in the uncuttable category are bottles having mouths too large or too small to accept the cutting apparatus, if you are using a cutting kit that requires attachment to the top of the bottle. The too-large category includes some of the most attractive specimens to be found in the supermarket, particularly in the bottled fruit-juice department. The too-smalls often are interesting bottles for seasonings, sauces and such. Too bad, but worth considering before purchasing a product simply for the sake of its otherwise desirable bottle.

If that seems like an awful lot of restrictions, be of good cheer! There is an abundance of wonderful, colorful, useful, desirable bottles left. Latching onto them is the trick.

WAYS TO COLLECT BOTTLES

Soliciting

Ask your neighbors, your family, your friends to save empty bottles for you. Before the look of compassionate bewilderment that will greet your request has time to congeal, tell them what you want the bottles for and take time to review the restrictions that might make a bottle uncuttable. No use wearing yourself out dragging home baskets and boxes of empties you can't use, and having some helpful soul clutter up the pantry with well-intended bottles only to be faced with the problem of disposal. And "thanks, but no thanks" can put a hefty strain on the ties of friendship.

A better source of bottles would be hotels, restaurants, bars, catering establishments, hospitals, school cafeterias and any other facility that principally or incidentally serves food and drink to large numbers of patrons on a regular basis. Empties invariably are a disposal problem in such places, and even if they aren't, your regular removal of them could be a well-regarded favor as long as you maintained a consistent collection schedule. A large caterer handling several affairs in the course of a weekend can come through with more bottles than you otherwise might collect in a lifetime. Hotels ditto. The corner tavern might yield full quart and larger bottles that you would encounter less frequently from private sources. The school or factory cafeteria is largely the province of waxed cardboard containers, plastic bottles, and aluminum cans, but any institutional food-service facility is a better possibility for large bottles and jars than would be my cupboard or your pantry. The problem is to establish a time and place for collection that is convenient to you and acceptable to your supplier. If the local bar doesn't get around to gathering up its empties until three a.m., you might want to think twice about rattling around in the back room, or rummaging through an alleyway only to find a bunch of ordinary green mixer bottles like those you could easily have creamed off your neighbor's patio at three thirty that afternoon. A busy caterer, rushing to clean up after a score of events, might not want you picking and choosing among the cartons of empties and might suggest you agree to cart off everything or not bother stopping around.

A hospital might not only yield food and beverage bottles, but also occasional gems in the form of medicine and chemical jugs. Ditto for laboratories, dry cleaners and pharmacists. It is best, however, to know what such containers previously held, since harsh alkalis and strong acids can leave imperceptible residues sufficient to cause skin irritation, unpleasant or even dangerous fumes, and possible "boiling" when the presumed-empty is immersed in water. If you are not absolutely certain of what purpose such containers were used for—and remember that the most recent use might have no relation to the original contents—then for the sake of your hands, your lungs, and your peace of mind, leave them alone and concentrate on bottles that are sure to be innocent.

Your local luncheonette or soda shop probably gets syrups and flavorings in large and useful bottles that would make worthy additions to any cutter's collection, and the ubiquitous "No Return/ Non-refillable" approach has come into effect in these areas as well as in individual packaging.

Shopping

Try the thrift shops in your community. Fancy wine bottles turn up in mine all the time. Try the genuine charity shops as well as the secondhand or junk stores. Charity-shop bottles are frequently washed and *sans* labels, which is a convenience to be further dealt with later. They sell at prices ranging from absurd (one dollar and up!) to forgettable (five or ten cents).

Cuttable bottles in interesting colors and shapes can be purchased in many antiques shops, too, and again at variable prices. Some antique bottles have surprising value to collectors and the going rate might seem a bit startling to the uninitiated with nothing more in mind than cutting that pretty purpled bottle into a hanging planter. With bottle collecting becoming a hobby of near-epidemic proportions and values of many desirable collectable bottles on the rise, antiques dealers and other vendors of used merchandise are giving increasing attention and space to their bottle displays. Certainly it makes no sense at all to destroy a fine antique bottle that might be worth as much as thirty dollars by cutting it into something that could as easily have been made from a brand-new, absolutely free "Federal Law Forbids . . ." bottle gleaned from the aftermath of some neighbor's annual Labor Day barbecue. *The Antique Bottle Collector** by Grace Kendrick contains not only a wealth of fascinating detail concerning old bottles but also features a complete price guide to current values. Since bottle cutting and antique bottle collecting are superbly companionable hobbies, this book makes a worthwhile addition to the bottle cutter's bookshelf and comes in handy when searching for bottles to cut. A price guide such as the one included in Mrs. Kendrick's book can help you avoid destroying an antique bottle that might have substantial value to a collector, while a little crafty comparison shopping can save you from paying a premium price for a readily available commercial bottle.

Flea markets, garage sales, charity bazaars and rummage sales —all can yield useful, inexpensive bottles that will suggest new and different cutting projects. Remember, though, when venturing into this territory, that wrapping service is apt to be a fairly haphazard business. So to be sure that you get your bottles home uncracked, unchipped and unshattered, you will do well to go armed with a sturdy shopping bag for carrying and a supply of old newspapers for wrapping. Remember too—don't worry, you will after the first such safari—that even a bunch of empty bottles can get pretty heavy in the course of a few minutes of carrying about. Use a double shopping bag, adding, if you can, one of those finger-saving wood-and-wire handles.

---

*Pyramid Publications, $2.95.

Scrounging

When you strike out to gather bottles from those vacant lots and dumps where abandoned empties glitter as enticingly as the fabled emeralds of El Dorado, take along a shopping bag and some newspapers *and* a couple of other pieces of helpful equipment that will make scrounged bottles a safe and sensible adjunct to your collection. You might not want to get involved with rakes and shovels which some serious collectors of old bottles carry along when setting out on a "dig," but take at least a length of sturdy doweling, or a pair of tongs—ordinary kitchen tongs, such as you might use to turn the steak, toss the salad, or grab a hot biscuit from the oven. You also could use the kind made especially to grip nursing bottles hot from the sterilizer. A sturdy dowel rod —even an old chair rung will do perfectly well as long as it is not too thick to pass easily down the neck of a bottle—or the tongs will save you having to handle dirty bottles and will enable you to pick them up untouched and to deposit them in your bag without having to worry about germs, insects, and other unpleasantness— including cutting yourself on an unsuspecting rim chip.

Insert the dowel into the mouth of the bottle and as deep inside as sensible leverage might suggest. Lift the bottle, still impaled

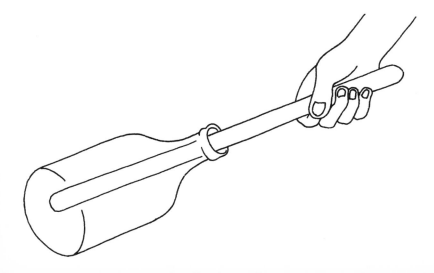

on the dowel, and slip it off into a plastic bag that you have been holding in readiness in your other hand. Remove the dowel, tie the bag closed and you have a neat, spillproof, germicidal wrap that will protect both you and your scrounged treasure until you can deposit the bottle directly into a waiting soak and scrub. You can do the same bit with tongs, which come in handy when a bottle you want happens to be playing ostrich with its top buried in the dirt. Of course you'll want to spill out any liquid—spirited, stagnant, or otherwise—but slip the bottle into a water-tight plastic bag just in case. A roll of large-size plastic freezer bags goes well into any bottle-scrounger's kit, together with a batch of those twist-tie fasteners that the manufacturer sends along with the freezer bags that I buy. Once your scrounged bottle is in its own plastic compartment, you can wrap it in newspaper and add it to your shopping bag or carton. You do need the extra insulation of newspaper around each bottle. Just once arrive home from a bottle search with a box full of broken glass, torn plastic and dubious liquid residues and you'll know exactly why.

Vacant lots are more apt to yield whole, usable bottles than will refuse dumps. "Take a walk on the Boardwalk" as they used to say in my old Monopoly game, to find pristine empties in the sand. In addition to "No Deposit, etc." some disposable bottles are marked "Don't litter," but a five minute shore-front stroll will make you wonder why the manufacturer wastes time with that ill-heeded nod toward environmental neatness. From a practical point of view, by cleaning up the place, you are doing something positive about pollution and getting yourself some fine free bottles into the bargain. Remind yourself of that, should some passing stroller look askance at you.

Wear a broad-brimmed hat if you are going to be out in the sun all day scrounging along a beach or in unshaded vacant lots.

A hat that ties on under the chin is less apt to blow away, or to fall off when you stoop to retrieve a bottle. And when you want to have both hands free to salvage and bag a find, a hat is a lot less troublesome than an umbrella.

Sunglasses are handy too. Not only against dazzle and glare, but also to protect your eyes from flying particles of dirt and sand, and the tiny insects that sometimes swarm in and around the mouths of discarded bottles.

Personally, I have to admit that just about the only thing I can manage to do successfully wearing gloves is to take off a pair of gloves. I have seen pianists wearing mittens bang out the Second Hungarian Rhapsody without missing a note. And yes, I know that surgeons do all their wizard-work with gloves on. Me, I'm just peculiarly uncoordinated; if there's work to be done, I must get my fingers on it or I turn out all thumbs — which is why I don't wear gloves when bottle scrounging. If you happen not to share my peculiar limitation, by all means add a pair of gloves to your equipment list. It could save you some skin, fingernails, and scrubbing.

Salvaging

Check around for local glass collection days and points in your community. The pollution fighters in your area are sure to have some sort of glass-gathering system underway. Maybe it only will be a couple of bins established near the town square. Or a full-scale, all-out, city-wide drive conducted with all the organization that the Boy Scouts or the P.T.A., the Lions, the Rotary or the ladies of the local garden club can bring to it. Whatever it is and whenever it is, there will be bottles aplenty contributed to it. And if you can convince the powers that be that you fully intend to launch a small recycling system of your own, you can gather an astonishing number of bottles by putting yourself in the right place at the right time.

I once canvassed a long line of cars waiting outside a Boy Scout glass-collection post and, garnering empties as I went, managed to fill my car by helping unload some of the others. This had the happy effect of providing me with a lot of bottles in a single stop and also substantially shortening the waiting line, which let the Scouts, their leaders and the people impatient to contribute bottles all get home in time for lunch.

When salvaging, however, it is important to establish that you fully intend to dispose properly of any unused glass, lest they suspect you of single-handedly trying to subvert their efforts.

Salvaging will turn up incredible quantities of bottles that you will not want, but it also will contribute plenty of useful multiples to your collection.

Most glass reclamation is broken down by color—clear, green, amber—and if you are interested only in acquiring bottles of a particular color, it is easy enough to post yourself by that bin and grab your treasures before they have a chance to join their shattered peers. I spent one salvage morning dividing my time among the three bins. I presided over the clear collection from nine to ten, the slowest hour, because I knew that clear bottles would be the great majority of the day's take. From ten to eleven, when activity and contributions picked up a bit, I stayed with the green bin, thinking that green probably would be the second most abundant color. The busiest part of the morning, from eleven to noon, I waited at the amber bin, because the heavier traffic resulted in more contributions in the least common color. Collection contributors usually will have sorted their bottles by color, which makes salvaging by color a lead-pipe cinch.

Oddly enough, like the proverbial housewife who spends two days straightening and cleaning her rooms so the place "won't be such a mess" when the cleaning woman comes, many of the environment-oriented glass contributors will make at least a modest gesture toward cleaning the bottles they are about to throw away. Perhaps because they have been hoarding bottles for as long as a month while waiting for the next regular collection, or while accumulating enough bottles to make a trip to the recycling center worth the time and effort, they find that giving each addition a fast rinse in clear water is a lot less bothersome than letting a bunch of mold-gathering, insect-attracting, sticky, dirty bottles clutter up the garage. In any event, many of the bottles salvaged from collection stations and drives will be happily free of the accumulation of wet leaves, grass slippings, coffee grounds, twigs and other less-wholesome plant and animal residues that so often characterize scrounged bottles. Which means that on a salvaging day you probably can get by with some newspaper and a couple of sturdy shopping bags or cartons.

CARRYING YOUR BOTTLES

Wonderful cartons for transporting bottles you have begged, scrounged, or salvaged probably can be obtained absolutely free from your neighborhood wine-and-spirits shop. The empty cartons in which the liquor store received its merchandise are sufficiently sturdy to sustain the weight of a dozen liquid-filled bottles, which means that they are not going to collapse under even two or three dozen empties. These cartons invariably will have been cut open along the top edges only, so that you will not have to worry about regluing or taping closed any risky bottoms or sliced sides.

And if the cardboard honeycomb that kept the original contents from cracking into each other has been left in your carton, it can perform the same happy service for the bottles you collect as long as you will settle for packing only twelve bottles to a carton. If you do, you can manage breakproof transportation without bothering about newspaper wrapping.

Those cartons, however, are less easy to carry than are the covered fruit-and-vegetable crates you might be able to charm out of your favorite grocer. Designed with corresponding slots to be used as finger grips, these boxes have strength and full-scale fitting covers that can do extra duty as auxiliary cartons if you happen across an unexpectedly generous bottle windfall. What they also have is an opening dead center at the bottom and top. Cover it with a couple of old magazines or a scrap of cardboard. And don't forget to newspaper your bottles before packing them.

ESSENTIALS FOR BOTTLE CUTTING

Oil

This is one item that you absolutely must have for successful bottle cutting. It is essential to the efficient use of the cutting apparatus, and I don't think any of the kits that promise to deliver "everything you need" actually includes it. Forgive the packagers this tiny inaccuracy and arm yourself with a small supply of oil. Here's an economy tip: You can use just about any oil that happens to be handy, even salad oil, mineral oil or baby oil—for that matter, even the oil in which you fried last week's chicken croquettes provided you strain out all the fugitive croquette crumbs. Regular household lubricant oil costs much more per ounce than

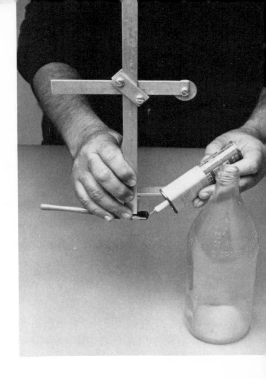

does salad oil, which you usually buy by the quart. Of course, you'll need only minute amounts of whatever oil you use, and you won't save enough for a mink coat or a weekend in Paris, but every little bit helps.

Glasses or Safety Goggles

Just to be on the safe side. Bottle cutting is one of the safest crafts, but there is the matter of glass dust, tiny particles it might be best not to hazard getting into your eyes.

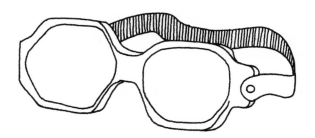

Finishing Paper

Your bottle-cutting kit may announce that it contains "everything you need." In a way it does, but in a very practical sense it doesn't. The quantity of sandpaper furnished with most kits is sufficient to finish about ten projects. Well, maybe fifteen. So, at the hardware store pick up some extra sheets of emery paper. Tell the clerk you want "wet or dry" sandpaper (you need waterproof sandpaper for reasons to be dealt with later; for the present just take my word for it) in grade 80 and grade 320. If your dealer cannot supply you with one or both, settle for something like grade 180, which will save one step in finishing your cut bottles but will also wear itself out a lot faster. One of the best of the bottle-cutting kits includes a meager amount of finishing paper, a shortcoming for which it compensates by providing a jar of miraculous grinding powder and a handy order blank for use in ordering more.

Candles and Ice Cubes

Short candles—five or six inches tall—and a supply of ice cubes should be kept in readiness for completing cuts with the heat-cold technique. You'll need some matches, too, of course, and a sturdy, squat candlestick. You don't want to use tall tapers or willowy holders, because you would then have to hold the bottle you were heating at an awkward, uncomfortable height. Ideally, the combined height of candle and holder should be between six and eight inches, which would allow you to rest your elbows on your worktable while holding the bottle just above the tip of the candle flame. As used in this process, ice cubes melt very quickly. So if you plan to complete many cuts, be sure you have a dozen or so cubes set aside for that purpose.

SOME USEFUL NONESSENTIALS

A Plastic Basin or Tub

For soaking and washing bottles, it's better than the bathtub or the kitchen sink. The absence of faucets, metal drains, hard surfaces and other invitations to broken glass gives the plastic tub a big advantage. The one I use has a slightly rippled bottom which helps discourage bottles from rolling into each other. If you want to leave a batch of bottles submerged overnight, the portable tub can be tucked away in a quiet corner while stubborn labels and grime leisurely soak loose. You won't have to fret about bits of foil and paper clogging the drain or about the water seeping slowly away during the night.

A Plastic Scrub Pad

Sooner or later you're going to encounter a bottle label that absolutely defies thorough removal. Reach for this handy little scrubber when you do. And don't worry about scratching the glass—it doesn't.

A Jelly-Roll Pan

To be useful for bottle cutting a pan should have a shallow rim —about one inch—all around. Most baking sheets or cookie sheets have an open edge at one or more sides, which rules them out for this purpose. An 11-inch by 16-inch pan of sufficient

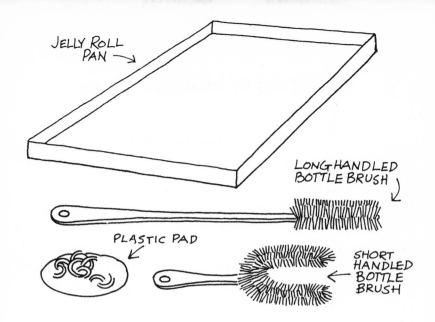

JELLY ROLL PAN

LONG HANDLED BOTTLE BRUSH

PLASTIC PAD

SHORT HANDLED BOTTLE BRUSH

strength not to dent or buckle easily, and having a depth of about one inch, can be used as a work surface for both the cutting and finishing steps. They should be metal; not Teflon-lined—no sense in paying extra for a nonstick coating you'd only ruin while cutting and finishing bottles.

Bottle Brushes

Have at least one brush with an extravagantly long and fairly flexible handle and a tuft of bristles at the nether end for digging out stubborn sediment and the like. A thorough soaking usually will suffice to clean all but the most difficult bottles, but have a brush on deck just in case. It is convenient, but not necessary, to have a smaller brush (for smaller bottles) and one of those old-fashioned vegetable brushes for digging out the last particle of dirt that might be lurking in design impressions and other such traps.

Cleaning Preparations

Ordinary household ammonia, liquid detergent and chlorine laundry bleach are useful for getting any kind of glass, from an antique Sandwich candlestick to an empty "No Deposit/No Return" cherry cola bottle, to come out sparkling like Cinderella's slippers. Have them on hand to use in *weak solution* according to directions in the next chapter. *Warning:* observe cautions given there or risk piercing, irritating fumes, tear-filled eyes and other unpleasantness that any sensible soul would prefer to avoid.

A Length of Broom Handle

Or any other cylinder of smooth wood about 8 to 10 inches long and about 1 inch in diameter. For finishing.

Paper Supplies

Paper towels are great for drying glass. You also will need some old newspaper for use in lining your cutting tray or covering your work surface. Newspaper is handy, too, for wrapping cut parts that are waiting completion.

That's really all you need, except for such finishing touches and accessories as will be dealt with in a chapter of their own. Take the least interesting of the bottles that you have collected, and let's get started. . . .

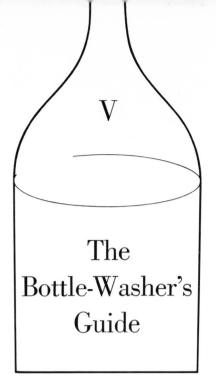

V

The Bottle-Washer's Guide

W̲ho needs to be told how to wash an old bottle? Who indeed! Yet there are a few good tricks that can save time and effort and money—and the disappointment of breaking a bottle before you get a good chance to go to work on it with your cutting tools.

One of the hardest things to remove from many bottles is the narrow metal ring that remains around the neck after one of those easy-to-twist-off caps has been easily twisted off. If you are planning to cut a bottle that wears one of these annoying bands, be sure to remove the band before going any further. Do this even if you are not planning to use the portion of the bottle that wears the ring. Most of those rings fit tightly and in spite of their feeble strength are difficult to pull off. The best way I have found is to grip the band with a pliers and give a snappy, twisting pull. Save the corks and caps unless they are shot—you never know when you'll need one to finish a project.

Get out your plastic tub and half-fill it with lukewarm water. It's a good idea to let some water fill each bottle as you immerse it. Hold the mouth of the bottle at water level, leaving a bit of space for air to escape, and wait until the bottle is sufficiently filled for the bottom not to float. This will not only keep the bottle submerged while it is soaking but will make it much easier for you to position bottles for maximum use of available space and keep the bottles from rolling around in the tub.

Once all your bottles are sunk, you can fill up the tub and go off and forget it for an hour, or an afternoon, or even a week, if that's the sort of person you are. Some labels will detach themselves almost instantly. Others will take a little coaxing. It is convenient to soak and peel several bottles at once, turning the entire washing process into a kind of assembly-line operation. Also it saves lots of water and cleaning preparations.

Foil decorations, labels and the like fall into two categories: those that will oblige you by floating off in the washing process, and those that won't. There are some labels that will, like an aging stripper, gracefully peel to a point and then refuse to budge, leaving some strategic covering stuck so tightly you'll think it had been nailed down. An extra soak sometimes will do the trick.

When it doesn't, you might try using slightly warmer water, raising the temperature gradually until the glue starts to soften.

When most of the paper, foil and the like has worked itself loose from the bottle, you might find that stubborn areas require extra attention. The plastic scrubbing pad—mine is called "Tuffy," but it's gentle as a lamb, obliterates paper and doesn't scratch glass—usually will serve to wear away any paper that hasn't soaked free. If stubborn kernels of glue persist, you probably can get rid of them with a fast rinse in warmer—even hot, you could risk it by this time—water.

ONE PART HOUSE HOLD AMMONIA   TO   ONE PART LIQUID DETERGENT   TO   ½ PART CHLORINE LAUNDRY BLEACH

ADD TO A LARGE VOLUME OF WATER

Ordinary household ammonia, liquid detergent and chlorine laundry bleach, combined in gentle proportions of one to one to one-half added *carefully and separately* to a large volume of water, make an excellent washing solution for any dirty glass. A celebrated antiques dealer who specializes in fine art glass first tipped me off to this magic elixir. She also told me about washing glass in a plastic pail in order to minimize the chance of breakage. I whipped up my first batch of ammonia-detergent-chlorine-and-water and almost asphyxiated myself in the process, but I got a prized Gallé vase to reveal two subordinate colors that I hadn't realized were there.

AN IMPORTANT WORD OF CAUTION: *Never add water to this*

mixture; add the ingredients to the water. And work near an open window. In that way you will save a lot of coughing, tearing and other unpleasantness. The small amounts of ammonia and chlorine that you will use become diluted immediately when added to a larger volume of water. Adding water to the full-strength liquids, on the other hand, risks piercing fumes, irritating splatters and similarly distressing consequences while the chemicals gradually are diluted. In any event, if you are contending with bottles that really are dirty, inside or out, you will find that they look better and are infinitely more pleasant to work with if you give them a bath in this solution.

Whip out your brushes to dislodge any stubborn deposits of sediment and soil lurking in the interior. It's best not to shake a bottle filled with even a diluted form of this solution. Getting splatters and sprays in your eyes is a definite no-no. Smarts like mad and could do even more hateful things.

Hard-to-reach or hard-to-dislodge sediment probably could be more easily cleaned once the bottle has been cut. But it might interfere with your ability to correctly observe certain steps of the cutting process if you plan to divide the bottle at or near the sedimented spot. In other words, if you're only going to chop the neck and shoulder off a bottle, you needn't spend half an hour trying to dislodge a crumb of moldy cork and some fuzzy grape pulp that looks as if it has been lying at the bottom of the bottle since Mary of Burgundy married Maximilian Hapsburg back in 1477. But if you're going to try to cut anywhere near the clouded area, take time to scrub it out.

Some books on glass cleaning and care recommend that you toss a length of chain or some fine steel shot into the bottle when washing one that refuses to come clean under normal conditions. Personally, I never have had to. Besides, I wouldn't have the nerve. And if I did, whenever I've run to the cupboard, two things I almost never find there are lengths of chain and fine steel shot. Braver spirits insist that it works. I'm willing to take their word for it and stand by my bottle brushes.

Finish with a rinse in clear water and let the bottles drip dry upside down.

You can upend them in a plastic dish rack, if you have one handy that doesn't happen to be full of dishes. Or if you have an old umbrella that's shot, but still has good strong spokes, you can impale your bottles on them and hang it up to dry, provided you position your bottles with nice balance. You can dry bottles upside down in a kitchen colander—the one you drain spaghetti in. You will find that if you leave wet bottles sitting upright on your windowsill (or anywhere else) the last drops of moisture almost never evaporate and can be quite confusing once the cutting business gets underway. Same problem arises if you try stacking your bottles in a wine rack, even as you might if they were filled. The angle usually isn't sharp enough to permit a good thorough drying job, and you will find anything from a few drops to a goodly puddle lurking in the bottle that you thought to be dry.

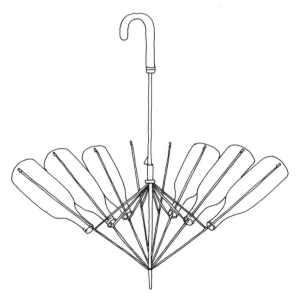

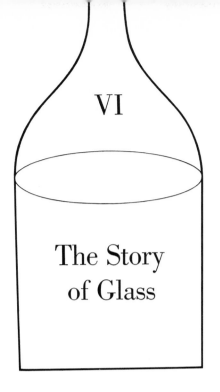

VI

The Story of Glass

Glass always has been thought of as a miraculous material. Since before the Christian era, it frequently has been treasured as a precious substance, worthy of being set in gold, and occasionally valued even more highly. The contradictory qualities of delicate transparency and durable strength have charmed artists and collectors since the age of the Pharaohs. In Imperial Rome, when vessels of glass were more highly prized than some fashioned from precious stones or metals, the Emperor Nero reportedly paid the equivalent of $2,500 for a pair of glass cups. In China, in the eighteenth century, the Emperor Yung Chêng charged the director of the imperial pottery to create porcelain copies of objects of the famous glass of Ku-yüeh Hsüan, which he greatly esteemed. For four hundred years the city of Venice exercised harsh control of the Murano glassworks and, in an effort to dominate worldwide production of glass, severely punished any artisan who revealed the secrets of the craft. One of the first manufactures undertaken in colonizing the North American continent was the production of glass beads for trading with the Indians who set great value on the glittering trinkets. From the late Victorian years through the first quarter of the twentieth century, which many consider to have been the great art glass era, in France, England and the United States, artists such as Louis C. Tiffany, Emile Gallé, Frederick Carder, Thomas Webb, Victor Durand, René Lalique and the Daum brothers captured and influenced the taste of the time from Victorian decoration through the sensuous appeal of *art nouveau* to the dynamics of *art déco* in glass articles of great importance and beauty that continue to be prized by contemporary collectors.

Oddly, the superb adaptability of glass to mass-production techniques caused it to become integral to social progress even as it increasingly became taken for granted. Molding and pressing were ancient methods of shaping and forming glass objects, but it was not until the second half of the nineteenth century that these techniques were widely applied to large-scale commercial glass production. According to Grace Kendrick, author of *The Antique Bottle Collector*, it was not until 1903 that machine-made bottles first became a reality, and only in 1920 that mechanical methods of bottle production were adopted throughout most of the world. With that, the glass bottle became a commonplace. The recent introduction of the "No Deposit/No Return" bottle went a step further and made it expendable. Yet the much-prized transparency that caused an emperor to pay a small fortune for a pair of glass cups still is present. And the color range would captivate the eye of any connoisseur.

Glass is a fascinating and contradictory material. Strong

enough to wall a skyscraper, it also can be so sensitive that the shock of a sudden temperature change will break it. Delicate as a soap bubble, it can nevertheless endure, rocklike, thousands of years of desert burial. It is the stuff of legends—Cinderella's fairy slippers, Alice's wonderful mirror. Or it can be the housewife's friendly casserole that hops attractively from freezer to oven with nary a crack of complaint. By the hands of a master craftsman, it can be carved like marble into creations of breathtaking beauty and power. It can be spun into shimmering silken threads to weave into inexpensive but luxurious-looking fabrics. Whether individually blown by an itinerant nineteenth-century glassmaker who would stop and knock out a sugar bowl or a jam jar to order for a frontier farmer, or mechanically stamped out by the gross in one of today's fully automated computer-controlled factories, every glass article holds something of the miracle of sands fused in the fire, of earth made transparent as water.

Certainly the noble lineage and notable properties of glass would seem to recommend for even the most humble examples a finale more glorious than the garbage dump, more distinguished than rejection or abandonment along a littered roadside.

Bottle cutting will give you a renewed appreciation of the beauty and versatility of this miraculous material as you explore new ways to reveal its multiple decorative and practical possibilities. You do not have to become a second Gallé to enjoy working in glass. The bottle manufacturer will have presented you with a finished piece of metal. Bottle-cutting equipment and a lively creative imagination are the only other essentials. You will find that you quickly develop a genuine feeling for glass, that you no longer simply see old bottles, but instead see a Swedish-modern-style cheese dome, a sparkling aquamarine candlestick, a puffy fruit-patterned sugar bowl and the beautiful, abundant materials from which they can be made.

I N D E X

Michael De Forrest is the author of nineteen previous books, of which the most recent is HOW TO BUY AT AUCTION, and has written the screenplays for three feature films. He also writes a monthly feature on antiques and collectables for *Newsday's* Sunday magazine, *LI*, and frequently appears on television to demonstrate and discuss articles from his personal collections of glass and porcelains.